i am the rage

D1403483

i am the rage

DR. MARTINA McGOWAN

Illustrated by DIANA EJAITA

 sourcebooks

Published by Sourcebooks
P.O. Box 4410, Naperville, Illinois 60567-4410
(630) 961-3900
sourcebooks.com

Library of Congress Cataloging-in-Publication data is on file with the publisher.

Printed and bound in the United States of America.
VP 10 9 8 7 6 5 4 3 2 1

To my daughter and my best friend, Amanda,
who listens to my stories and poems with great
patience, gives honest critique, but more importantly,
lends unwavering support to my projects.

To all the Mothers and Fathers of Children of Color.

To my father.

Contents

I Am the Rage   1

Forever Lost between Sunlight and Shadow (for Breonna)   5

Motivated Forgetting   9

Human Enough   11

Navigating This Hazardous Terrain   15

Benediction Number 9   17

There Is Too Little Time   20

America's Postpartum Depression   22

In My Rearview Mirror   24

America's Music   28

Numb to the News   30

Rhetoric   35

We Still Stand (Noble and Proud)   37

A Shocking New Race War   39

How Could We Not Have Appreciated That   42

Why We Beat Our Children   47

A New Song   50

Not Again   52

Be Careful What You Ask of Me   54

Traffic Stop   56

How You Hate to Rape Me   61

Tale of Two Georges   65

America, Something Is Wrong   68

Juneteenth   71

We Are Alike, You and I   75

BIPOC   78

Spoken Words Fail Me But…   80

Cultural Upheaval   82

Today, I Cannot…   83

What Sadness We Carry in Ordinary Times   88

Acknowledgments   93

About the Author   95

America, once again, has civil and racial unrest with protesters flooding our cities, calling for justice for all, with people being detained, brutalized, and murdered on the streets, as well as in their homes, without the benefit of due process. **These and other heinous crimes are sadly not new to our nation, nor do they show any signs of ending.**

I am the American Heartbreak –

The rock on which Freedom

Stumped its toe –

The great mistake

That Jamestown made

Long ago.

—LANGSTON HUGHES, 1951

I Am the Rage

I Am the Rage

I am the rage, roiling just beneath the surface
I am the dream deferred
    Again
I am the promises kneaded and repeated
But never kept
I am the air between light and dark
Fueling flames that burn,
but can neither be consumed
nor satisfy its own abiding hunger

I am the glowing embers you continue to poke and prod
    with meanness
That bubbles over onto the streets
I am the ravenous appetite to destroy
Something
Anything

I am the ever-present clanking chains
In the belly of the cargo hold
Struggling to love myself
A thing You have taught me to loathe
I am the dismal days and inky skies

I am the niggardly feeling that there is not enough
Will never be enough
Money
     Land
          Freedom
               Education
                    Life
To satisfy us all

I am the outrage that flares every time you say something
     foolish like
"I thought you were already free."

I am the disappointment that breathes hot and silent
Every time I am dismissed
Discharged
Dishonored
Cast aside
Counted as worthless or meaningless

I am the melody that lies inside every Negro spiritual
That sings praises of diminishing hopes in this life
And a brighter, fairer world in the next

I am the mother who wields the belt that cuts both ways
that beats my children
in hopes that You will spare their lives

I am the salty tears of anxious mothers
Frightened each time her child crosses the threshold
Praying for a return that is not guaranteed
Like payment of some impossible garnishee on the lives we
    want for them

I am the furthest point from You
Thrashing about in the sea of doom
    Gasping for air

I am the dark fiber that runs through our shared history
that will not allow You to forget
    A constant reminder to us both
that I can never go home
        Can never find home

I am the rage, running unbridled through the streets
I am the fire this time
I am the rapacious thirst seeking justice for all
On these dusky days and obsidian nights

I am the rage that lives within the powder keg
   of unfulfilled lives
Awaiting the spark

I am the rage
I am the lost sheep
I am the muted prayer that we will
   see each other clearly one day

Forever Lost between Sunlight and Shadow

For Breonna

Caught between sunlight and shadow
Yesterday she lived carefree
Perhaps again tomorrow, she thought
Except that

This day she was murdered
In her home
Asleep
Defending her love
Defending her peace
Thinking she was free from the shackles and the shadows of
  history and hate
But we are never free

Yesterday she went to work
And helped people
And laughed
Remembered bright days
And smiled her beautiful, luminous smile

Yesterday the shadow had not yet issued the "no knock" warrant
Yesterday the shadow that haunts us all had not yet battered
down her door
In the middle of the night
Where she slept
Thinking she still belonged to the sunlight

Yesterday she spoke with her mother
Transported people to the hospital
Held their hands and shared in their moments of pain and
darkness

Yesterday she ordered lunch with her friends
Yesterday she planned on going out Friday night
And maybe Saturday night too
Stop downtown to pick up some barbecue
Thought about what she could learn at work
To improve herself
To earn more pay
To rise through the ranks

Yesterday she did not know that the shadow was so very, very
   close
      In fact
Only a few hours and eight bullets away
Yesterday she thought she still had time to bask in the glow of a
   thousand tomorrows

Yesterday she lived at the right address
Not a great address
But her address nonetheless
Where she could walk outside
And laugh with friends
And hang on to the bright promise of hope

Yesterday she did not know that
The wrong address would become her address
That the person she would be mistaken for would already be in
   jail
That there would never, ever be another tomorrow

Yesterday she did not know
That her light would be erased
That she and the shadow would finally become one

Yesterday her calendar was full of hope

Promise packed to the margins
But no more
Never again to think of tomorrow

Her light, brutally extinguished by the shadow
Bent on destroying us all

Motivated Forgetting

Whips, chains, and shackles
Mark the apocalyptic turn of all darker peoples
Whips we continue to use on ourselves in corralling
Our unnatural naturally violent nature
Or so You tell us

The intensity of life has not changed in these 400 years
200 years as freed-men and freed-women
Or, only free-ish
Our lives only remaining physically intact if we can continue to
  outrun
The slave patrollers and the police

There is no afterward for such brutal and bestial treatment
Unless you consider heaven
Maybe

There is only motivated forgetting of the cruelty endured all
these centuries
There are fragile hopes that die
On the fluttering wings of butterflies
But there is no life, liberty, or pursuit of happiness
Here

Human Enough

With diminishing confidence
We send out our heart-sensors
To try to remember where our children are supposed to be
And at the same time
To touch the God that binds us
To each other

The God that binds us to each other
Tries to break that awkward silence now filling our homes
As we review our day's journey
And begin to wonder where our children truly are
And if they will return

If they will return unharmed

Once again on this freedom's eve

In a world that denies the proclamation of their
  emancipation

Reminding them daily that they are not free

To be

To love

To breathe

To live in peace

To have the time to reflect and contemplate

To reflect on the days that we have lived

And contemplate what the tomorrows may bring

But we already know

Tomorrow will bring the same fear

The same fear that we are unequal

That we are still three-fifths human

On a good day

And on a bad day

We are not human at all

    Never completely whole people

    Never entirely free from bondage

    Never free from violent assaults on the body and the mind

The violent assaults of the mind and the streets

Force mothers and fathers

To our knees

To hold watchnight service within our hearts daily

To daily hold watchnight service in our hearts

To bring our beautiful three-fifths human children home again

Singing songs of sorrow

Songs of oppression

Slave songs

Sometimes we simply rock and moan

We stand, we kneel, we pray

Sometimes in our private prayer closets

But always in our hearts

Always from our hearts

We reach out to the God that keeps us

And binds to each other

Bent low before the One Source

Backs broken in prayer and supplication.

Backs broken in prayer and supplication

Tonight and every night is watch night vigil for my child

Prayerfully asking

On this night

Will my child be human enough

To return to me unharmed

Navigating This Hazardous Terrain

We navigate this hazardous terrain
Trying to advise You that there is indeed a struggle
There is a gap

Seeking a seat at the table
To plead our cause
When You claim there is no cause for alarm
  No brutality
    No violence
      No otherness

To seek restitution for our lives distorted by
A people who would douse our incandescent spirits
Take away our languages
And rename our tribes

A delicate and deliberate climb
Out of the slimy pit
Continually living on the edge of change and promise
Never fulfilled

Surviving a waking nightmare

Beseeching You to break the shackles

You refuse to acknowledge even exist

Holding back the violence inherent in unrecognized anger

Which will rise to bloodshed again and again

Because the struggle to bridge the gap

is way too real

And far too much to contain in this puny vessel

This mortal flesh

Always just a hairsbreadth away from death

As we continue to navigate this hazardous terrain

Benediction Number 9

I must to let you go, my friend
Although *friend* is not the right term
My acquaintance is perhaps closer than mark

Floating in the outer rim of your influence and sight line
The smallest speck of consideration in how you think and see
Letting go of the noose that binds us
to what we could have been to each other
Teacher
Mentor
The peace we could have brokered
The good we could have done
Together

For months, or is it years, I have tried to whitewash
the frayed baggage of the beliefs
you carry
And cherish
And cling to
Beliefs I thought we could investigate together
And learn from each other

But your vile language
And contemptible moral superiority
Can no longer be tolerated
And, in case you did not know,
Tolerate is not a word of friendship

In this moment of crisis
Which should mark a time of change
You go back to your safe space
And you announce that you are done with trying
Done with conversation
You would have joined us in the struggle but...

But the protest did not go the way you wanted
The rage spilled over from cracked cups of peace to looting and
    burning
As it always does

Your insolence and blindness
Can no longer be sanctioned by my heart
The underlying, all-too-familiar cadence of this equality dance
has grown laboriously burdensome to my spirit

I wish you well in protecting your moral high ground

But I now know

I can no longer call you friend

If I ever could

There Is Too Little Time

There is too little time to teach our children
That there is no after
To this ubiquitous feeling that
Life is but a stream
Trailing from our bodies
Almost unseen

There is too little time to spoon-feed our children
Giving them false hope and false hype while
Trying to convince ourselves that
The world can be full of wonder and fair
But they are not free to hold it

There is too little time to teach our children
That the fairy-light touch
Can quickly turn into a bite from a policeman's club

There is too little time to teach our children
To say "Aye" to all that life has to offer
And to every passing whim
Knowing it will not be offered to them

There is too little time to teach our children
To fight to keep their spirits free
The insignificance of a hope for tomorrow
Managing the lies of the apostles and apostates alike
The sweetness of oranges
The tiny moments that make life sweet
The defiance built into their very DNA

There is too little time to allow our children
    to be children

America's Postpartum Depression

We can hear it in the streets
The agonizing wails of postpartum depression
    of child abandonment
From a nation trying to circumnavigate its responsibility
For a problem she has brought to her own shores

Snatching away the teat from those left wanting
Eroding all trust
Leaving her bastard children vengeful and resentful

The reddening earth from each battle we fight
Trying to bring about some reckoning, resolution, fairness
Serves as a metric to our growing enmity
Which has few boundaries

Children, who in Your self-righteousness
You have carelessly fathered and left behind
Nor wish to claim as Your progeny
With mothers no one loves
And whom You no longer wish to recognize as Your passion

The music has gotten away from the melodist

The dance has devolved into a tormented and ragged musical

Which we must reenact every few decades

Coming no closer to resolutions or solutions

In My Rearview Mirror

In my rearview mirror

I hear the sirens long before I see the lights
Before the vehicle comes into view
Is it a fire truck?
An ambulance?
         Or a police car?
Two of these cause no trepidation
No quickening of pulse.

When I look again in my rearview mirror
I see the police lights
Rushing toward me
Sirens blaring
Getting louder
Closer

I am certain they are not coming for me
Well, reasonably certain
I have done nothing wrong

I go over my internal checklist

Speed limit – ok

Correct lane – check

License in purse – yes

Registration and insurance in the glove box – yes

Everything I might need to reach for clearly visible – yes…

   I think

Tags up to date – probably

All should be well

But I know what I look like

I know how the world sees me

I know that sitting or driving in my car I fit the proverbial
    profile

    Black

        Too dark sunglasses

           Dreadlocks

              Sex, unknown

Probably singing too loudly, even though my windows are
    closed

Out of fear

I slow down

I drift further to the right

I try, with some sense of urgency,

To blend in with those driving much too slowly

I struggle to get my breathing under control

Loosening my grip on the steering wheel

Checking to see if there is anything else that looks suspicious
    on the front seats

Even though I know in my heart and in my logical mind that

Nothing and everything can be suspicious

They finally pass me by

I almost drop my head to the steering wheel in relief

A trickle of sweat running down my back

Because of the fear

The real fear is this:

One day this will not end so well.

America's Music

As I drift off to sleep
I hear and feel a concussive blast which shakes my house
And I know the streets are alive again tonight

Pulsing with
Fires and violence
Tears and screams
Sweat and force
Fists and batons raised

I live upstream from tonight's violence
So it probably will not touch my home
Nor take my life

We can be assured that little will be achieved
save venting of outrage
We will still gain no freedoms
We will secure no justice

The ephemeral hush is interrupted by a staccato of gunshots
That pierce my heart
My psyche is startled
But hardly shocked

The flaring of nostrils
The rhythmic chants
The stamping of feet as they struggle to push the march
    forward
The beating of fists against riot shields
And clubs against heads

Bass notes played by helicopters not too high above us
By pilots who have not yet realized
That this is all part of the native song of America
Our national anthem of greed, violence, suppression, and
    oppression
To which we have all learned to dance and dutifully accept
Until the next time

Numb to the News

The news has become so repetitious
It has become almost boring
Esoteric
Unbelievable
    Unless you are of color

Little girls with their molars coming in
Sleeping on grandma's sofa
    Dead

Sleeping with your Boo in the middle of the night
Anticipating your morning shift
    Dead

Skittles
    Dead

Violin
    Dead

Hoodie

    Dead

Suspect handcuffed

Running backwards

While holding a weapon on two officers

    Dead

Suspect handcuffed

In the back seat

Of a patrol car

Shoots himself in the head

    Dead

Traffic stop

    Dead

These and many more deaths can be dismissed with a single
   phrase
"I was in fear of my life"

Perhaps we should pass out cards
to facilitate and streamline the news reporters' jobs,
As well as the angst and the agony that follow

No repentance for crimes

No remorse for loss of lives

Presumptive guilt

Injustice meted out with "evidence" as flimsy as cirrus clouds
Not to be too seriously investigated

Presumptive guilt

Presumptive penalty
　　Death

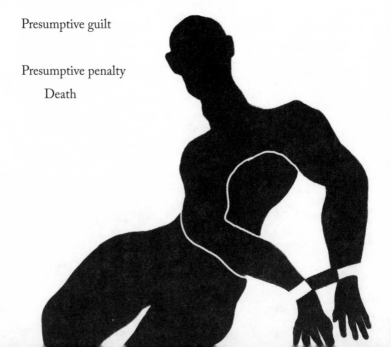

Snake oil salesman telling us it is all in our imagination

We are blowing things out of proportion

We are wrong about
Brutality doled out by bullies
Seeking to extinguish the brands called "Black" and "Brown"

Seeking to eradicate "others"
To bolster their own insubstantial pride
And reassure them of their moral superiority

Because
You cannot be superior without someone else being inferior
You cannot have a top with no bottom

Up with no down

Upper hand without a lower hand

Excellence without "less than"

Nobility without serfs

Rank without file

Insider without outsider

Us with them

Masters without slaves

Rhetoric

The constant din of rhetoric
Rotting away even the vaguest of hopes
That things will change
Get better

Police strutting like cocks in a henhouse
Champing at their bits, clutching their clubs
waiting for the curfew hour, and the beatings to begin
Acting out orders embarrassing even to the Germans
While others kneel and walk with the protesters

Numbered quotas of arrests and beatings
Solidification of hard hearts
Tightening of helmets and flak jackets

The erosion of freedoms
By plague
And the wellspring overflowing from a deep well of loathing
The broken and boarded-up windows of the dreams of others
While our blood stains every sidewalk

Prayer warriors offering thanksgiving

for having come this far

By faith

Which is where exactly?

Clinging again to the dubious threads of anticipation

For another watered-down version of slavery

Which should appease us for another decade

It is a ghostly form, an apparition

That walks among us

One that can never truly become whole or visible to all

While this river of blood continues to flow

In every city and lives in every battered soul

We Still Stand (Noble and Proud)

Trapped beneath the floor
Underneath the glass ceiling
We can never break our stride
Nor sow our downcast spirit
While we wait for the breakthrough

Whether a tramp strolling by
With all belongings in a prized supermarket basket
Or a stranger preaching on the street corner
"The End is Nigh!"
Deemed cagey by the hue of his skin
Rather than his message or the state of his mind
Or a bird boy checking out his charges in the park
Accused of harassment and molestation

Abundant as the unplowed fields of our 40-acre "gift"
Rising and rising again like a zephyr
Undaunted by Your desires to erase us

Grateful that our forebears possessed indomitable spirits

And the fortitude to believe and hold fast

To their dreams of freedom

Of better tomorrows

But at a heavy cost

Their lives

And the dearest things to us/them

The lives of their children

We continue to traverse this land

Pushing against the fetters of Your mind

And the cramped lives You have carved out for us

No matter our station nor lot in this life

We still stand as noble and proud people

Unbowed and unashamed

Knowing that

You may kill a few of us

But You will never destroy us

A Shocking New Race War

This newest war on racism is new to You
Not to me

You have discovered that you do not know me
Trying to learn more about me and my "kind"
Stuff I have always known

Angling to increase Your count
Of how many Black bodies
You can call friend
Even though we are not
Never have been

Fawning over us like new expensive toys You bought Your
    children for Easter
Picking up and putting up with
Choosing us as the cheapest, droopy puppy You took pity on
    while shopping at some mall

Continuing to shove and steer us into roles

Ill-suited for us both

The proverbial square peg into the tiny round hole of Your
design

I need you to stand with me and walk beside me

Not rushing ahead of me

because You know better than I

what should happen to me next

The road is unfamiliar to You

But not to me

I have traveled this road many times

Literally spent the days of my life upon it

    Like some worthless coin that goes in and out of fashion

I lick the wounds from the last two, or is it three, race wars

    For I have lived a long time

And try not to remember that You were the one

Who fell behind

every time

And then dropped out of the race

Without a backward glance

Abandoned the war

Leaving me dangling in the breeze

Alone

Again, naturally

Outside Your world

in the cold

With yet another heavy noose coiled around my neck

    Holding me in place

How Could We Not Have Appreciated That

How could we have judged ourselves so harshly and so poorly
So poorly that we did not recognize
Ourselves as beautiful
As graceful
As stylish
As magical
And unique

Nightly nestled between my mother's knees
As she ruthlessly corralled my "nappy" and unmanageable hair
Into neat cornrows
Determined to plow the paths straight
So that the rows remained intact for at least 24 hours

Gently applying Bergamot
Less so the stinky Glover's Mange
To force little seedlings to grow
How could we not have appreciated the beauty and art of that

Preteen years aligned with
An overwhelming desire
to have "big girl" hair
Sunday morning
Snuggled between my mother's breasts
Seated by the stove
The dreaded curling iron moving deftly
To make ringlets
That would barely last through church

Chastised for moving too much
Trying to preserve the tops of my ears
To only end up with
Burnt knuckles instead

With ribbons and my finest clothes
My Sunday-best
Topped off with patent leather shoes
How could we not have appreciated and celebrated the beauty
    and the art of that

Many years and dollars later

Hair

Mutated

Weaponized

Revolutionized

And much to my mother's dismay

Transformed back into "nappy" hair

Cake cutters and Afro Combs

Adorned the largest crown the little seedlings could produce

Beautiful in its message

Soft as lamb's wool in its texture

Colorized to highlight its singularity

I wore a blond streak in mine

Individualized to sing each souls song

How could we not have appreciated the beauty and the art of
    that

Greasily Gerried

Traveling back in time

To ringlets that would last for months

Braidable

Moldable

Almost too long to manage

Who would have thought all this could be birthed from such
paltry seedlings

How could we not have appreciated the beauty and the art of
that

Now braided

Or locked

Or plaited

Or extensioned

Or Afroed

Or dyed

Or fried

Sending new messages to a deaf world

A message that says

We are indeed individuals

Each one of a kind

And we may wear our crowns of hair

Our crowns of beauty

Our mother's glory

And God's glory

In any manner we choose

Because we are beautiful

Too long languishing and not seeing

Ourselves as we are

How could we not have appreciated the beauty and the art

The beauty we continue to make of every part of our bodies and
   our lives

In spite of,

Or is it because of,

All we continue to endure

How could we not have appreciated the
   beauty and the art of all that we are

Why We Beat Our Children

Born into a world that understands the gross mishandling of
  people
As property
Importing forms of punishment
We ourselves disdain

Dealing with the pain in our own microcosms
Trying to right a long and terrible wrong
Born with the invisible psychological scars
Matching the physical scars on our ancestors' backs

How do you keep a child safe and alert
How do you corral a free spirit
Without destroying it

How do you clear away the cobwebs of disobedience
The randomness of thought
How do you manage the natural disagreeableness of teens and
  preteens
And spawn a new and improved version of the thing you love
  most

You use what you have learned

From my grandmother telling her daughter

    To go get a switch

To her

Telling me

    To go get the belt

The emotional anguish of that long walk

To get the instrument of your own torture

To the trauma indelibly marking

A relationship that could have been different

Maybe

How do we try to keep our children safe?

We use what we have learned

We beat them

We restrain them

We hold them in check

So that they learn to obey commands

Especially from white police

But we cannot have it both ways

As we eventually learn

We cannot have the warm and cuddly relationship presented on
    TV

And have children we are certain

Will return to our arms safely

So we pass on this hateful system of crime and punishment

Praying that they can see our love and agony beneath

And that they will find a new way to protect their own children

Or

Maybe

The world will change

And we will not have to work so hard

Trying to keep them safe

But probably not

A New Song

Orphaned by a nation that castigates us at every turn
Looking to any individual acts of violence as
A justification for a condemnation of an entire race

How do we get to middle ground, the golden mean
To find a way forward
A way out of this never-ending cycle of outright war and
unfettered bloodshed
A way out of this spiral toward the death of all things good
Forward to a way of peace
Armistice
Without swallowing the bitter pill of business as usual, which
only brings us back to strife

How do we turn down the violence of us versus them

Them versus US

Mortal enemies on this battlefield of life

What is the escape route from this labyrinth of animosity and
remorse

No one will yield

who holds the secret unction that can heal the scars of a
crippled nation

How do we find the pathway to a new story

And stop the reiteration of the old

The story that has never furnished us with real hope for a better
tomorrow

And explodes or collapses on an extraordinarily regular and
predictable path every time we play that old record

Who will hear a new story

A new narrative

A new anecdote about how we can live in actual, factual
harmony and altruism

Before we destroy ourselves.

Not Again

I do not crave Your patronage
As You suspect or hope

While You grow weary of looking for plausible
Ways to reach down
Dirty Your hands
To help me
And my kind

I do not seek Your ingenuity or input
Into what will make my life better
Or make it more like Yours
While You test these newly-formed but tenuous bonds of trust

I refuse to be a party to Your abortive attempts to educate
    Yourself
At my expense
To understand the language of back-lancing scars
And spirit-crushing humiliations
To obtain knowledge I already possess
To help you feel better about Yourself

I will not enter into that turnstile of time
With You another time
Only to once again find myself ultimately lost
Locked inside the same old prison
Alone
Again

What should You do
What do I suggest You do
Find one child
Lock yourself into his or her life
Feel the darkness with them
Educate them about the ways of Your world
And help them navigate it

For the days are sad
And tomorrow is guaranteed to no one
Especially not to a Black child

Be Careful What You Ask of Me

As we paddle life's stream from one crisis
To the next just around the bend
You ask me to travel with You
On this epic adventure to understanding me
Us

While this seems to you to be a harmless pursuit
And something we can revisit on a regular basis
Keep in mind the hidden damage to my heart and psyche
As we paddle into a dark world
Unreal to You
All too real to me

It is hard to blithely revisit a history never acknowledged
Never cradled in the bosom of Our nation
Never offered comfort
Or care
Or recognition
Or rectification

There are so many blind spots just outside Your peripheral
    vision
It makes my spirit weep
And my bones ache
At the thought of the retelling of the story

Perhaps I can be one of the pillars in repairing Your knowledge
    deficits
But I must also protect myself in the process
You will not
You cannot see it
Unless I tell you about it

You cannot feel the pain
Nor the weight of histories we carry
Your history
Unless I tell you about it

You cannot stand in my place
Or walk in my shoes
We both know this
But
I will try my best to tell you about it
Again

Traffic Stop

Traveling cross-country during the lockdown
Beautiful landscapes
Interrupted by a traffic stop

Pulling out of the traffic
My gut knows what this is about
Although my white friend will take more time
To process it

She pulls to the right shoulder
Once she is certain he is following us
He walks up on my side
The passenger-side
And looks in the window
And tries not to stumble over his words
Once he is aware that only the passenger is Black
And not the driver

Stuttering through

"Well, you were following too closely"

License and information about the rental requested

She digs out her license

I do not

I hand him the paperwork for the RV

He invites her back to his car

So he can write out a warning

Gregariously saying

"No ticket this time

Watch your spacing

Keep it two to three seconds' distance"

She goes back to the car

Stands on his driver-side

He chats her up

About the cost of the van

How he needs a vacation

How she looks relaxed

Writes out his bogus warning
"10 miles under the speed limit
All paperwork in order
Following too closely"

Three days later
Yes, the time it took Christ to rise from the dead
She has an "aha" moment
An epiphany

Replaying the event out loud
Rereading the warning
She realizes the stop was not about her
Or about doing anything wrong

It was about what he thought he saw
Through our windshield
Black people
On the road
Spending money
Being carefree

But I know
Even if she doesn't
That we are never free

There is always someone
Who thinks we are doing the things
They should be able to do
And by so doing,
Deprive them
Driving cars
They should have
Going to schools
They should be in
That we are living their best lives
And feel obligated
To terrorize us
Out of having fun
Remind us

Hound us back to our proper position
Send us back to their plantations
To do their work for them
Take back the things we have earned
And own
Returning everything to them
Even though they are not entitled to it

It is the existential and everlasting rut
In which we all live
As unending as the rivers of time and history

And yes
Unbowed
We will endure it
Knowing that
Freedom
Opportunity
Exemption
Will only ever touch a few of our lives at a time

How You Hate to Rape Me

Your actions and your leering gaze
Where your friends cannot see you lustily looking my way
Make a lie of every negative word you speak to or about me

You call me nigger, whore, dog
Yet you long to lay cradled inside me

You long to take hold of flesh that was never yours to possess
To poke and prod
To seek love and finding none
You seek to ravage, consume, annihilate

Oh, to feel the smooth insides
To touch the heart and heat of power
That you can neither define nor imprison

You with your clan of friends, holding me in place

Demanding that I move for you as if you were an authentic
   lover

You plunge your corrupted flesh into the secret spaces

you allegedly despise

Yet yearn to embrace

You take me at gunpoint

Painfully pressed against my skull

Knives held against my neck

Flashing your torchlight and badge in my face

As justification and reminders (to yourself) of your corruptible
   power

You spill the terror of your seed upon the ground and on me

Seeking to water down what?

My race

My color

My self

Your craving for what I have

What I am

For what you can never be

Diminishes you in the light of day and shows you have no true
power

Derogating my estimation of who and what you are

I bear the shame in the public eye

While you hide yours in the recesses of your perverted heart

Who is the punk?

The bitch?

The beast?

Who is the coward here?

Because

after all

I am still here

Living in the light of life

While you continue to tuck your sins away in the alcoves of
your spirit

Knowing fully well that you are less than a man

Less than human

And although you may be able to periodically terrorize me

Rape me

Even kill me

You can never own me.

Tale of Two Georges

Leaning over my body
Whose name is George
Learning my oath to hold all life sacred
Except for that George that the policeman forgot was under his
    knee
While he was conversating
And protecting and serving

Apologizing for the violations
I must perform to learn
The building blocks
And substances
That make us all human
And not "other"
As our society dictates

Periodically asking for help
So that I do not cut the wrong venous conduit
prematurely
Offering thanks for a life
Lived on the shoulders
Of those who have been cut down prematurely

My lab partner leaves and I am elated
To spend time communing with George unencumbered
And exploring the gifts he has to offer me

Shutting out the noise of the world
And its violence
I learn to listen

In the silence
Between the words
Between the heartbeats
For all that is unsaid

I learn to hear the pleas of others
When they do not know the lingo

I learn to read their expressions

See their almost-hidden pain

Interpret body language and movement

To comprehend what the body seeks to teach me

There in the silence

In the cadaver lab

I learn to translate and transmute all of these little "nothings"

Into relief for others

There in the silence

I learn my job

My profession

My definition

My job is to listen

I listen

If only that policeman had been taught to listen

That other George

Would still be alive

America, Something Is Wrong

America, something is wrong
We are the exotic and perverse fruit that hangs from those
Sweet, sweet Magnolia trees
Reminding You of a home filled with love
And reminding me of your malignant hate

America, something is wrong
We are the products of an American education system
Schooled at underfunded dropout factories
Struggling to touch a life perceived
But still dangling just outside of our grasp
And still living a hard and dichotomous life

America, something is wrong
We are the victims of Your deadly and quick judgments
Judgments with neither the ring of justice nor mercy
Only character assassinations

We are the many generations left behind

Widows and widowers who have lost their spouses

Yet there is no name for a mother seeing her child lying dead in
the street

Although it happens with regularity

And yet

We remain bitter, bold, and only partially broken

Living a bicameral existence

Because we understand Your intentions for us

Even if You will not speak them clearly

America, something is wrong

You are afraid

Good so am I

This is a fear you have

Bred

Engendered

Cultivated

Nurtured

And now You cringe at the thought and sight of what You have
finally birthed

Painstakingly brought forth by the midwife of time
A bastard child who hates You as much as You hate it

An imperfect reproduction of You
A lot less white
Bearing Your family name

A mongrel of Your shame
The shame You try to hide away from the clear light of reality
by using faulty history
Born with a caul over its face
Because it was never meant to breathe
Shame at what You have conceived in the shadows of Your heart

America, something is wrong
We are the walking reminders of an assortment of sins
The sins you now seek to turn into corpses at every opportunity

America, something is wrong
And until you can shake free from your own shackles of shame
You bind us all together
In a bizarre dance of rejection and reconciliation

America, something is wrong

Juneteenth

From Lincoln to Granger
To the enslaved, imprisoned, and powerless
A two-year journey lost on the lips of a nation still embattled
And now a holiday to be celebrated by all

Freedom
A single word of curse and blessing
But the blessing was thwarted

The delay of a government agent killed on the way with the
   good news
or
Withholding the news until the final slave-driven cotton
   harvest can be brought in
For profit

What did this new freedom bring

Slaves made free

To do what

Absolute equality of rights and rights of property between
  master and slave

New relationships forged between employee and employer

Free but not free

Slave but not Freeman

Now free in the country we do not know or understand

Freedom that left broken families – broken

Broken tongues and languages – lost

A broken spirit

A new status on paper

Or not

Of falsities that our lives would be the same

A nation bathed in the idea that whiteness is superior

That it is the final goal

The ultimate state of being

A new life without simple protections afforded most Americans

We celebrate the end of human trafficking

Except it wasn't

Making an unhealthy contract

A perilous and corrupted deal with the devil

Yielding futures that have remained little changed

A new life coupled with complaints

Complications

Complicity

Conflagrations

Confusions

Counterfeit protection

Because someone must still be the lowest caste

We see with clarity

That the languorously moving march to freedom

With laws that wholly protect all citizens

Has brought about de-evolution of the American spirit

This involuntary arch

Brings us into a new era

But by our own choosing

Also drags with it broken shards of past centuries of hate

So that we can continue with the detrimental obsession that
   rightness is whiteness

Two years and now two centuries later

Our lives remain virtually unchanged

The patrollers are dressed differently

They have traded in their tattered rags for riot gear

Swapped out their whips for tasers and bullets

But our lives remain unhelpfully and unhealthily
the same

We Are Alike, You and I

You and I are so alike
It scares you

A mysterious blend of several African nations
And multiple European countries
Coalesced to make you and me

We are sentenced to be locked into invisible battles
Fighting on two fronts
A plague of disease
A plague of the heart

In your blindness
You do not see
Or you do see me and fail to understand me
Or understand and refuse to acknowledge me
That the upward or downward trajectory of this nation
Our America
Depends on the fate you have in store for me

Is there a retrospective guide we can point to
For finding the way forward
Have we passed the mark of turning or the point of tipping
Lost in our never-ending whorl of degradation and denigration

We are alike
You and I
As you shove me aside
And lock me down
You do the same damage to yourself
Everything you have done to destroy me
You have done to your nation
Yourself
Your children

You cannot shoot me without seeing me
You cannot push me without touching me
You cannot spit on me without droplets of the same venomous
    slaver finding its way back to your face
You cannot hate me without seeing that beneath the color, I am
    you
You cannot lynch me without feeling the bite of the rope on
    your dirty hands
You cannot shun me without leaving a hole in your world

A testament to what your forefathers made

The strongest of us

Each in our own way

And as a testimony to the acrimonious history we share

We will come for you

Not with clubs

Or tear gas

Or firebombs

But with words

We are alike

You and I

And until you see this with clarity

This grand democracy we call home

This nation

Will never cease to burn

In the fires of hatred

Licking and caressing its wounds

Nursing its hurt pride

Shoring up its damaged spirits

We will be with you until the end of time

BIPOC

Sitting on a powder keg
Or in a cage
Waiting for the spark to ignite
Still trying to interpret the illegible runes of
How Black and Brown peoples are ineligible for a life of
  Liberty

Doors bolted shut
To keep us from
Stretching too far
Or reaching too high
Or overstepping the prescribed lines demarcated in the ever-
  shifting sands
The amorphous borders of the lives we are allowed to live

What will it take
How many lives need to be lost
How much blood has to be spilled
To buy back our freedom
A thing, like our bodies, You had no right to own

And as You push back

Ever-faithful in reminding us that we are not human

Not really like You

Can never become You

Even though we have no desire to be

Now calling us BIPOCs

A different kind of beast

A euphemism

An abstraction that simply means

Not white

Or not white enough

Spoken Words Fail Me But...

Although words often seem to fail me when I try to speak
The writing still comes by instinct
An instinct long-buried
Not safe for polite society

Breaking out of the cookie-cutter mold of being a well-
    mannered possession
A slave to what makes others feel comfortable
I plumb the depths of a pain we are afraid to speak
And take repossession of a spirit lost in financial serfdom

Temporarily casting our outward-facing selves into
    obsolescence
Acknowledging the absolute logic of our tears
and agony
and outrage
Showing the unseemly details, the horrific density of the lives
    we live
We inadvertently open a new chapter of misery and degradation
And open old, unhealed wounds
Again

Our true spirits struggling to wriggle out of its safe space
No longer hidden from a world that wishes us
gone

But take heart
We will disappear from your sight again

In a few months
This broken world will return to business as usual
And our ambiguous losses will still be lost
Our freed spirits will once again
be locked in amber
Awaiting release in another age of outrage

Cultural Upheaval

As we ponder the next steps in our cultural overhaul
The scholars and artist souls are set ablaze
By a deluge of material that keeps us one step
Away from both insanity and utter despair

The crude and rude treatment repeatedly visited
With a violence and a vengeance
that leaves us breathless and confused

We go through the mechanical motions of our crafts
And inevitably come crashing back to the earth
And struggle with the mundanity of everyday life

What makes us crafters special
Also makes us strange
Riven from the hoods of our hearts
We remain intertwined with the struggles of our people

Alas, we too fit the profile
And will, in time
Be destroyed

Today, I Cannot...

Today, I cannot come out to play with You
It simply hurts too much

Today I cannot push down the pain
The hurt
And the grief
Of the disheartening losses and daily devaluation of human
  lives

Today I cannot write or paint without crying
Filled with rage and fear because it never ends
Because it never ends
Because it never ends

Today I cannot go exploring with my guild-mates destroying
  monsters
Because
Apparently, I am a monster
  Or I look a lot like one

Today I cannot stop thinking about
Ahmaud (jogging)
Breonna (sleeping)
Steven (going to work)
George (knelt upon)
Chico (raising his hands in surrender)
And the injustices we have all endured

Who is next?
Me?
My children?
My nephews?

Today I cannot act as if I am one of You,
And that the world is not on fire
I am not one of You
I am one of "them"

Today I cannot pretend that I have never been

Detained

Accosted

Mistaken for someone else

Belittled

Overlooked

Bypassed

Segregated against

Denied access

Required to show extra ID

Watched the light go out in someone's eyes when they discover

that I am Black

Aware of the rank odor of fear exuding from my pores

Felt the constant need to look over my shoulder

Assess my surroundings

Living in a world where I am more terrified of dying while

doing ordinary things

Than I am of dying of this deadly plague

Worried and constantly checking my posture, my tone, my

expression so that I do not

Seem too large, too dark, or too threatening

Even though I am righteously angry and grieve for people who

thought there was still an inherent promise of tomorrow, or

some other (fucking) fairy tale

Today I cannot

Paint in bright colors while the world is locked into struggles of

Black and Brown and Racism

Blue and Red

Nor write the tortured verses of Haiku,

Without mentioning the black and blue hues of my pain

Or act like the world makes sense and appear to be well-

behaved

In a world that looks at me

and sees something distinctly "other" and/or "less than"

Something in desperate need of annihilation

Maybe tomorrow I can come out to play with You

Hiding behind the fraudulently color-blind screen

But today

I cannot bear it

What Sadness We Carry in Ordinary Times

What sadness we carry in ordinary times
Deep within our breasts
Our hearts threatening to burst

What sadness we carry in ordinary times
Told to breathe
It will make everything better or, at least, make it more tolerable
And gaining no relief
    When we say we cannot
Breathe inside this thick and foul fog of hatred

What sadness we carry in ordinary times
When we hold vigils to honor our dead
Being held in check by people dressed in riot gear
With tear gas bombs, flash-bang grenades, pepper spray, and
    bullets
Real bullets
While we hold poster board and cardboard signs
as our only shields against mutilation and death

What sadness we carry in ordinary times

Beaten with state-sanctioned clubs

Electrified and stunned into submission with taser guns

Punched with clenched and outraged fists

seeking a target to shatter

Lit up with rubber bullets

Because we are not happy

And we are outside our own homes when the sun retreats

What sadness we carry in ordinary times

When the hot wax of candles drip onto our hands

Reminding us that we are

    Still

    Alive

        Regrettably

What sadness we carry in ordinary times

Releasing balloons to honor the fallen

Attempting to release our pain into the firmament

Only to find them trampled in the streets a few blocks away or

   lost at sea

And we still carry the pain

What sadness we carry in ordinary times

When we reach out to the cosmos thinking we too are one with

   it

Discovering that we are instead

     an unfortunate parody of mixed but not blended peoples

Vilified by all

Trying to raise a thin wheal of hope for our children

What sadness we carry in ordinary times

Because

     No matter how gruesome the travesties

     How egregious the atrocities

     How ludicrous the explanations

     How high the body count

And

     even though we STILL, STILL, STILL cannot breathe

These are,

after all,

     for us,

only ordinary times.

Acknowledgments

To my daughter and my best friend, Amanda, who listens to my stories and poems with great patience, gives honest feedback, but more importantly, lends unwavering support to my projects. To her daughter, who reads with me, introducing me to new writers, and makes the best faces when she does not like something.

To my father, who taught me about love in the short time we were together.

To Mary Anne Radmacher, for her encouragement, resourcefulness, friendship, and holding my feet to the fire.

To Sweetie Berry (and her family) for being friend and strategist.

To my writing group, Údar Anam Cara, for sharing their work while supporting mine.

To everyone on the Sourcebooks team: Dominique Raccah, book publisher, for taking a chance on a first-time writer; Meg Gibbons, my editor, for making the process simple; Todd Stocke, editorial director, for his editorial comments and suggestions; and everyone else involved with birthing this first book, even though I do not know your names...yet.

To my extended family, friends, and coworkers who have supported me knowingly and unintentionally.

About the Author

Martina McGowan, MD, is about effective engagements in life. A physician (gynecology) who has spent a lifetime engaging formidable opponents, she has been a victim of and an advocate against social, racial, and sexual injustices, a participant in school desegregation and integration, and a physician serving women who have been victims as well as heroines in the war on women. Effectiveness means pushing through glass ceilings and perceived limitations of others. Whether conversation is about social and racial injustice, personal development, spiritual enlightenment, or her grandchildren's favorite books, she's about becoming involved wherever she finds herself. A writer, a potter, an artist, a leader at work and within her community, Martina believes in the example of decide, learn, do, improve as you go. She enjoys traveling, reading, and speaking, as well as copious amounts of laughter with family and friends. She feels that the most valuable skill in life is learning to listen.